MW01147018

THE
GHOSTLY TALES
OF
PRESCOTT

Published by Arcadia Children's Books
A Division of Arcadia Publishing
Charleston, SC
www.arcadiapublishing.com

Copyright © 2022 by Arcadia Children's Books
All rights reserved

Spooky America is a trademark of Arcadia Publishing, Inc.

First published 2022

Manufactured in the United States

ISBN 978-1-4671-9879-0

Library of Congress Control Number: 2022933034

All images used courtesy of Shutterstock.com; p. 58 Chris Curtis/Shutterstock.com;
p. 82 Thomas Trompeter/Shutterstock.com; p. 96 Pamela Au/Shutterstock.com;
p. 104 Charlotte Evelyn/Shutterstock.com.

Notice: The information in this book is true and complete to the best of our
knowledge. It is offered without guarantee on the part of the author or Arcadia
Publishing. The author and Arcadia Publishing disclaim all liability in connection with
the use of this book.

All rights reserved. No part of this book may be reproduced or transmitted in any form
whatsoever without prior written permission from the publisher except in the case of
brief quotations embodied in critical articles and reviews.

Spooky America

THE
GHOSTLY TALES
OF
PRESCOTT

ANNA LARDINOIS

Adapted from *Haunted Prescott* by Parker Anderson and Darlene Wilson

arcadia
CHILDREN'S BOOKS

ARIZONA

CALIFORNIA

NEW MEXICO

3

5 7

11 9
2
6 4
1

8

10

PRESCOTT

TABLE OF CONTENTS & MAP KEY

Yavapai Courthouse

Introduction

Prescott, Arizona, is full of history.

The story of this frontier town began in 1863. That's when explorer Joseph Walker and his party of men searching for gold arrived near the headwaters of the Hassayampa River. Walker was a famous scout who was known for leading the first group of settlers over the Sierra Nevada Mountains.

Walker and his men worked quickly. On May 10, 1863, they adopted laws governing this new mining district, and the town of Prescott was born.

This frontier town was once the capital of the Arizona Territory. The wild west town, known for its gold and silver mines, attracted both miners and bandits to the area in hopes of striking it rich. These men spent their time and money on Whiskey Row, until the great fire in 1900 burned the rowdy entertainment district to the ground.

And all of that history means Prescott is also full of ghosts!

A walk around Courthouse Plaza is a great place to begin your search for Prescott ghosts. Most of Prescott's best known haunted locations are within walking distance of the square. Stop in at the Palace Restaurant and Saloon, which is known as the oldest business and the oldest bar operating in Arizona. Some say it is also the most haunted place in the Grand Canyon state! Pop into the hotels around the square. You might catch of glimpse of a few former visitors who never checked out!

Ghosts seem to be everywhere! Whether you are at the museum, the theater, or just strolling down the sidewalk, there is a chance you could encounter an otherworldly entity. This frontier town is filled with frights!

Turn the page to meet a few of the spine-chilling specters who haunt Prescott. That is, if you dare!

Home of the Toughest (and Spookiest) Customers

The famous Palace Saloon on 120 South Montezuma Street is the oldest business on Whiskey Row. The first saloon on this site burned down in the Sherman Block Fire on February 14, 1884. It was rebuilt with a stone foundation and an iron roof, so people claimed it was fireproof. But the that was not the case.

On July 14, 1900, the Palace Saloon burned to the ground with the rest of Whiskey Row.

As fire tore through the buildings on Whiskey Row, the patrons who were drinking inside the Palace Saloon quickly gathered what they could and took it across the street to the Plaza. Men ran out of the building with their arms filled with liquor bottles, parts of the bar, and anything else they could carry. While the town was in flames, the Palace bartenders kept pouring drinks for their patrons.

The Palace Saloon was once again rebuilt, this time better than ever! When it opened its doors again in 1901, it was described as "an elegant pleasure resort." The saloon was built with the finest materials and modern luxuries, which were rare at the time in Arizona.

People flocked to the Palace Saloon. Some left earthly traces of their presence, like the rowdy cowboys whose bullet holes can still be seen in the ceiling of the historic building. For others, their presence in the saloon is not as easy to see, but it certainly can be felt inside the building. Their presence is so strong that many think the Palace is the most haunted place in Prescott.

The sign outside of the Palace Saloon says, "Serving Arizona's toughest customers since 1877." If you've visited the popular tourist attraction, you have probably noticed Annie. She is the mannequin that is displayed at the top of the stairs in the dining room. The statue is dressed in frontier finery and gives visitors a reminder of the saloon's early days.

Everyone knows that mannequins cannot move by themselves. Annie is just like every other mannequin. She cannot move—at least not when people are around. Once the Palace is closed, that is a different story!

It seems once humans have left the Palace for the evening, Annie is known to move around the balcony. The owner discovered that the statue moved several different times while the saloon was closed. One time, Annie's head was turned to face the dining room. Another time, Annie was spun around and was facing in the opposite direction she had been the day before. The owner was certain one of the employees was playing a trick on him. He decided to check the security cameras to see who was moving the statue. While watching the security footage, he made a spine-chilling discovery.

No one was touching Annie when the saloon was empty. Well, at least not anyone who could be seen. In the footage, Annie was seemingly moving on her own. He watched the film of the statue's head move, but there wasn't anyone else there. He was stunned! How could this happen? It seems as if there are two otherworldly explanations, and both are terrifying. Either a ghost is moving the statue, or the statue can, somehow, move itself. Both options are too scary to consider!

Whatever is moving Annie, it is not alone in the building!

There are claims that the ghosts of men from Prescott's history appear in the saloon on occasion. Witnesses have seen the apparition of the long dead former mortuary owner, Frank Nevin, seated at a table playing cards. Long ago, he and the sheriff, George C. Ruffner, were playing a high stakes game of poker at the Palace. Luck was not on Nevin's side that night. He lost his mortuary business to Ruffner in the game. Some believe his spirit returns to the saloon in hopes of playing one more hand of poker with Ruffner to win back his mortuary.

Unlike Nevin, not all of the Palace's ghosts can be seen. Some of the spirits might be trying to recreate a time when the Palace was a rough and rowdy saloon. Without warning, people have seen chairs tossed across the room by an unseen being. Bottles fly through the air seemingly on their own, and then shatter when they hit the ground. Perhaps these spirits are reliving a raucous bar brawl from the past?

The Palace's spirits also like to make their ghostly presence known in the women's bathroom. Stall doors will bang open seeming on their own. Lights will go on and off, despite the fact the light switches can only be accessed inside a locked case. Some terrified visitors have even reported orbs flying straight at them!

Fortunately (for you!) the spookiest part of the building is off limits to guests. It's the basement.

Those who enter the dark, empty space have a

sense of foreboding. There isn't much down there anymore, except a storage area and a few old jail cells that were used when new cells were being installed in the courthouse. Those sensitive to the paranormal report that the energy in the basement is heavy. Some have had a hard time breathing while touring the eerie space.

Unfortunately for some Palace employees, their jobs sometime force them to work in the basement. One young woman spent a great deal of time in the basement taking care of merchandise stored in the underground rooms. Her duties at the saloon changed, and as a result, she no longer needed to spend more of her work shifts in the basement.

One day, she needed to go into the basement. It had been months since she last been downstairs. She ran down the steps to collect some merchandise she needed.

The young woman quickly grabbed the items she was looking for and made her way back up the stairs. As she headed out of the basement, she suddenly felt pain in her torso. The skin on her chest and stomach hurt. She looked down at her body to see what happened. She could not believe her eyes. There were multiple fresh scratch marks dragged across her skin.

She could not understand it. Nothing touched her, so where could these scratches have come from?

One of the managers at the Palace had a suspicion that something supernatural may have occurred. He called local paranormal expert, Darlene Wilson, to check into the strange event.

Wilson saw the mysterious scratches on the young woman. Then the two of them went into the basement together to try to get to the bottom of what happened. While they were down there, they were able to detect unexplained temperature fluctuations in the rooms. They also captured photos of a few metallic orbs in the underground rooms. Both of those signs are thought to be evidence of an otherworldly presence. But nothing happened to the young woman during their investigation.

At least, until the two started making their way out of the basement. As the pair were talking, Wilson noticed angry, red scratches rising on the young woman's chest. Just like the previous time, no one had touched her, and she did not seem to feel anything as the scratches appeared on her skin. Seeing the scratches appear on the woman's skin, Wilson decided she needed to find out what was happening in the basement of the saloon.

After the completion of Wilson's paranormal investigation, she concluded that there is a spirit that dwells in the basement. And that spirit might be very lonely. Wilson thinks the spirit might have liked having the young woman around and missed her presence in the basement. Could those scratches have been the result of the lonely spirit reaching out to the young woman and trying to keep her in the basement with him? Wilson thinks that is exactly what happened.

With all the eerie events that occur at The Palace, it is easy to see why many in town

think the saloon is the most haunted building in Prescott.

People come from all over to marvel at the bullet holes in the ceiling and get a taste of what the Wild West was really like. But those tourists who enter the famous building might get more than they bargain for—and that seems to be just the way the spirits like it! Go if you dare, but keep your eyes open. No where is off-limits for the ghosts that have made the Palace their home.

CHAPTER 2

Missing at Matt's Longhorn Saloon

When you were a little kid, what did your family tell you to do if you got lost? Were you supposed to wait until you were found? Were you supposed to ask an adult to help you? Something else? In Prescott, there is one child still searching for her family.

There is one ghostly little girl who seems to be lost at Matt's Longhorn Saloon located at 112 South Montezuma Street. You might wonder how a little girl managed to find herself at a lively saloon known for its live music performances. Perhaps the child connected with the property during an earlier time?

Back in the day before the building was used as a live music venue, it was a store called D Levy & Company General Merchandise. The store closed in 1934 and has been a saloon ever since.

Inside the ladies' room of the popular music venue, there have been sightings of the apparition of a young girl. The otherworldly girl will approach women in the bathroom and ask for help. The girl says that she is lost and needs to find her mother. The women usually agree to help the lost child. Soon after the women start to look for the girl's mother, they discover that the child has vanished. Concerned, the adults who tried to help the girl search the saloon high and low looking for her, but she is never found. The truth slowly dawns on the helpful women. The child they had encountered wasn't a living child. They were talking with a ghost!

No one knows who the little girl is, or what happened to the mother that she is still searching for in the building. That lost little spirit might be behind reports of other paranormal occurrences in the building.

Visitors have witnessed the bathroom door locks moving on their own. Could that be the work of the child? A security guard told of a time he felt a tug on the leg of his pants while working at the front door. When he looked down to see who was trying to get his attention, no one was there.

Was this also the lost little girl? It could be this little girl's family told her to find a police officer if she got lost. She may have mistaken the man's security outfit for a police uniform and approach the guard for help.

Who the child is and how she got separated from her family remains a mystery. But this might be a good time to go over what you should do if you ever get lost with your family. You don't want to end up with the same sad fate as this child—forever lost and searching for your way back home.

The Terrifying Theater

If you've been to the Prescott Center for the Arts on Marina Street to see a play and thought it looked more like a church than a theater, you were right! The building is now a great place to catch a show, but when it was built in 1894, it was the Sacred Heart Catholic Church and Rectory. The final service in the church was held in 1969. Since then, the building has been a place for the community to enjoy the arts.

It is also the home of quite a few ghosts!

Those who spend time in the theater, or the old rectory, which is now used as the office and the dressing rooms for the actors, have grown accustomed to some unusual happenings. It is not uncommon to experience strange noises and unexplained knocking sounds that are believed to be the work of otherworldly beings in the buildings. The shadow of an unseen entity is occasionally spotted dashing across the stage, making itself known to those with watchful eyes.

They might be hard to spot, but these restless spirits aren't shy. They are also known to mischievously turn lights on and off on the unsuspecting visitors to the theater to make their presence known.

It seems paranormal activity in the building is most likely to happen when someone finds themselves alone. When the building is empty, there have been reports of hearing the murmur of many voices coming from the walkway between the theater and rectory. Those who have experienced it say it sounds like a large crowd of people, all talking at once. Each time someone hears the puzzling sounds, they bravely investigate the theater. They search for a radio left on or unexpected visitors. But no matter how hard the person looks, no source for the voices can be found. At least nothing the eyes of the living can see.

Who, or what, is responsible for these eerie happenings? It could be one of the two apparitions that regularly show themselves in the theater. No one knows who they are, but the staff at the Prescott Center of the Arts say a ghostly woman they call Sophie regularly makes herself known. Her laughter rings out from the second floor. Sometimes, she can be heard singing old-time gospel music. Maybe this giggling ghost was a member of the church choir while she was among the living?

Also seen in the theater is an unnamed young boy dressed in old fashioned clothing. Little is known about him, but he lets the staff catch glimpses of him in the early morning hours before the sun rises.

The ghosts might let the staff see and hear them, but they save their REALLY spooky activity for children who find themselves alone in the theater. On several occasions, children said they interacted with one of the ghosts who haunt the theater.

One young girl told her mother that she had a conversation with the ghost! The ghost joked with her, telling the girl that "the best part about being dead was seeing all the shows

for free." But, their conversation wasn't all fun. The ghost warned the girl to be careful. The entity told her that among the ghosts, there was a demon in the theater! A chilling message, indeed!

Another child who encountered a ghost had a less pleasant experience. The young boy was performing in a show at the theater. He seemingly disappeared from backstage. When he missed his cue to go on stage, people began to worry. They searched for the boy everywhere. They eventually found him, safe but startled. The young actor was hiding because he had seen a ghost. It terrified him so much that the only thing he could think to do was to run as far away from the eerie vision as fast as he could!

Perhaps the most bone-chilling experiences in the theater happened to a cleaning woman who would arrive at the theater before dawn. One morning when she was in the building alone, she heard a voice coming from the empty main theater. She paused to see if she could make out what the voice said. She heard her name being spoken from the vacant room. The unseen entity called her name again and again. Needless to say, she did not enter the dark theater!

But that's not all! Whatever haunts that building wants this cleaning woman to know it knows her name. More than once, when the cleaning woman was sweeping the dressing rooms, the ghost let her know she was not alone in the room. As her broom pushed the dirt and dust from the floor, she swept the pile of dirt toward the door of the room. When she was finished, she bent down with her dustpan in hand. She started to scoop up the pile of dirt, she saw something that stopped her in her tracks.

She saw her own name, traced into the pile of dirt she just swept up.

Just who lingers in the theater, and why spirits are bound to the theater remains a mystery. The otherworldly beings seem to want to have contact with the living. What are they trying to tell us? We may never know.

But one thing seems certain—you do NOT want to be caught in that theater alone. Not ever!

The Eerie Elks Opera House

No one argues about whether or not the Elks Opera house is haunted because everyone knows it is! The only thing people debate is the number of ghosts that haunt the historic theater. From the mysterious tug on a lock of hair to the phantom flushing of toilets, the spirits that inhabit the theater are an active bunch. Some claim to have heard the sounds of operatic singing echoing through the empty theater late at night. And believe or not, that might be the least scary thing that happens in the very haunted building!

Perhaps the best known apparition is the one that the Elks Opera House staff have nicknamed "Fillmore." The spirit presents itself as an adult male. Sometimes, the ghostly figure is clad in all black. At other times, people have spotted him wearing the clothes of a cowboy. Just who this spirit is remains a mystery. But, the ghost did give a clue to his identity late one night.

Once, when a cleaning lady was working in the theater by herself, she spotted the ghostly figure of Fillmore. To her amazement, the spirit spoke to her! The apparition told her that he thought the name the employees had given to him was "cute," but Fillmore was not his name. He told the woman that in life his name was

Robert. He revealed nothing more about who he was or why he remains in the theater. And so, the identity of the ghostly man continues to be unknown.

Another strange sighting occurred when the theater was being remodeled around 1980. While construction work was being done in the theater, a few of the workers heard the tinkling sound of glasses clinking together. They stopped working so that they could discover where the delicate sound was coming from. When they looked up toward the ceiling, they could not believe their eyes. The ghostly form of a young girl was swinging from the chandelier! While the transparent little girl was swaying through the air, the glass crystals hanging from the light fixture clinked against each other. Which is exactly the sound that the construction workers heard!

Could this playful, ghostly girl be the same one who is fond of gleefully giggling in the theater? Many have claimed to hear the sounds of a small child laughing when they have been in the theater. Those who have heard the laughter have looked for the source of the sound, but they never find it. Maybe this is part of a hide-and-seek game the spirit is playing with those who visit the theater?

Some believe the unseen, giggling child is a little girl who is rumored to have fallen from the balcony many years ago. The girl did not survive the fall. But, if the legend is true, her spirit lives on in the theater.

During the 1980s, a cheeky ghost started bothering visitors to the women's restroom. More than one person has claimed to have been visited by a ghostly presence while using the center stall in the bathroom. One shocked lady said she was using the toilet when suddenly, the door unlocked itself and flew open! Fortunately, she was alone in the bathroom when it happened, so no one saw her in that uncomfortable position. Well, except for the ghost!

The spirits in the theater seem to like playing in the bathrooms. The toilets are known to flush on their own. Water faucets are turned on and off by unseen hands. But, the ghosts' mischief is not limited to the bathrooms.

There have been countless reports of lights turning themselves on and off in the theater. Unaccounted for foul odors will occasionally fill the nostrils of those who visit. The source of the stench can never be found. Many believe the mysterious stinky smells are signs of an otherworldly presence.

People have also reported hearing disembodied footsteps throughout the building when they are certain the building is empty. Even more chilling are the reports of the sounds of muffled conversations coming from vacant rooms.

Perhaps most frightening of all are the reports that people have been touched by unseen spirits in the theater. Some have reported feeling an unseen hand push them. Others claim to have felt someone pull their hair. When the person turns around to confront the offender, they find themselves alone.

If all of that was not enough proof that the Elks Opera House is haunted, in 2018, Southern California Paranormal Research and

Investigations came to the theater to gather additional evidence of paranormal activity in the building. The ghost hunters were in luck! They managed to capture otherworldly voices on their EVP recording equipment. (EVP stands for electronic voice phenomena. Some people believe spirits can talk to the living, but we cannot hear their words without using special recording devices.)

Later, when the group decided to take a break to eat their evening meal, they left their recording devices on when they left the building. Just minutes after the group left the empty theater, something unexplainable happened. Not a single living soul remained in the building, yet somehow the lights in the theater turned on.

The strange phenomenon of the lights turning on without human intervention was caught on camera. If it was not something otherworldly that turned the lights on, what was it?

Why is this theater so haunted? No one really knows, but few who have visited the theater doubt there is paranormal activity in the historic building. It seems all of these ghostly encounters make it hard for the theater to hang onto employees. One employee revealed that after the janitorial staff begins working at the theater, "we get a lot of them that won't come back."

I can't say I blame them. If even HALF of what people have reported about the Elks Opera House is true, I'm not sure I'd be brave enough to be in there by myself at night. How about you?

The Macabre Masonic Temple

The old Masonic Temple building at 107 North Cortez Street was built in 1907. It was the gathering place for Prescott's Freemasons. Freemasons are men who belong to an organization that dates back to the Middle Ages. The four-story building is no longer the headquarters of the club, but the building is still an important historical landmark in the city.

And it is haunted, but not by the Freemasons.

Some think the building is haunted because the property used to be the location of the first courthouse in town. Not only was the building used as the courthouse, it also served as a jail, a meeting hall, a church, and most chillingly, a place where prisoners were executed.

Today, if you go behind the Masonic Temple, you'll find an alley, but back in the 1867, it was a fenced yard where prisoners who were sentenced to death breathed their last breaths. Most of the prisoners who were executed there are believed to have been murderers. Over the years, many men swung from the end of the hangman's noose on the property.

If you believe the tales, it would seem that the spirits of some of those executed prisoners still linger on the land. It could be their untimely deaths made it difficult for the spirits to cross to the other side. Perhaps the fact that

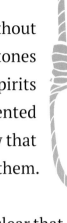

the executed men were buried without ceremony and have no headstones or grave markers make these spirits restless. Or, maybe these tormented prisoners want to let the living know that executing them did not get rid of them. No one knows.

Whatever the reason is, it seems clear that the spirits remain on the property. And these spirits are known to interact with the living!

Ghost tours and other groups who want to interact with spirits often visit the alley behind the building in hopes of having a paranormal experience. The ghostly entities that remain on the property rarely disappoint! Many visitors have reported feeling a tap on the shoulder, only to turn around and find no one there. And some have felt more than just a ghostly touch. Late one night a young woman reported being pinched on the leg when visiting the alley!

Shocked, the woman simply could not believe a ghost was able to pinch her. She didn't see anyone, living or otherworldly, touch her leg. But she was not convinced that there wasn't some logical explanation for the twinge she felt on her leg. Puzzled, she decided to return to the alley in the daytime to see what, if anything, would happen.

As it turns out, sunlight did nothing to deter the spirits in the alley. The ghostly being that pinched her the night before let the woman know, for certain, she was not alone. As she walked through the alley, she was pinched again! When she felt that sharp squeeze on her leg for a second time, she decided to get out of there and never to return to the property. Two pinches were plenty for her!

The alley is not the only place where restless spirits are found on the property. Specters linger inside the building as well.

The spirits are most active in the nighttime. They are well known to the cleaning staff who come to the building long after the businesses that operate inside the old Masonic Temple have closed.

While the cleaners scrub and dust, they hear the sounds of banging and doors slamming from the upper floors of the empty building. This experience might sound scary, but it happens so often, the cleaners have gotten used to the spirits crashing around the building at night.

But it is not just unexplained sounds, sometimes the spirits in the building show themselves! During one late night cleaning session, a cleaning man saw a woman enter the bathroom on the floor where he was working. There was nothing unusual about the woman. He did not even give her a second glance.

He decided to wait until the woman came out of the bathroom before he started cleaning it. He waited and waited. She still didn't come out. So, he waited some more.

Tired of waiting, he asked a cleaning woman working with him to go into the bathroom and check on the woman he saw enter the room. The cleaning woman walked into the room and found the lights were off and all of the bathroom stalls were empty. There was not a living soul in the bathroom.

When the man found out the bathroom was empty, he was confused. He was CERTAIN he saw a woman enter the bathroom. No one came out of the bathroom. Where could she have gone?

The cleaning woman just smiled at the man. She had a lot of experience working in the old building. She was aware of the paranormal activity that happened in the Masonic Temple.

The woman knew the man had probably seen a ghost. Finally, she said, "No worries, it happens to me all the time."

If you are looking for a ghostly experience in Prescott, the old Masonic Lodge might be the place to go. Whether you are inside the building, where the ghosts can be heard, and occasionally seen, or you're behind the building among the spirits that are able to touch you with an unseen hand you are bound to have a bone-chillingly good time. That is, if you dare . . .

The Gunslinger's Lament

Have you ever been curious about the building known as the Knights of Pythias building? When it was built in 1895, the citizens of Prescott were very proud of the three-story, forty-six-foot-tall structure. After all, at the time it was the second tallest building in town! The only building that was taller was the courthouse.

Back then, people talked about the building because it was tall. Today, they talk about it because it is haunted.

Many believe the spirit of James Fleming Parker haunts the Tis Art Gallery on 105 South Cortez Street. If you believe the stories, his restless spirit has been roaming the building since 1897.

Parker was born in California in 1865. By the time he was fifteen years old, he was an orphan who was doing time in San Quentin State Prison for cattle theft. This was the first of many times Parker would find himself behind bars.

After Parker was released from prison, he made his way to Arizona. At that time, he was working as a cowboy but he hadn't given up his life of crime. He was still rustling cattle.

On February 8, 1897, Parker and an unknown number of accomplices robbed the Atlantic and Pacific Train. Things did not go as planned. One of the accomplices was shot and killed during the robbery. Parker was able to flee the scene, but he was empty-handed. The law was on Parker's trail, and he was arrested within the week.

Parker sat in a Prescott jail awaiting his fate. He didn't want to spend any more time in prison. He began to plot his escape.

On May 9, 1897, Parker and a few other inmates saw their chance to break out of jail. The men overpowered the Prescott prison guard. The caused such a ruckus that the jail break could be heard throughout the building.

Popular Assistant District Attorney, Erasmus Lee Norris, raced down the stairs and into the room where the men were fighting the guards. It was then James Fleming Parker sealed his fate. Parker shot the twenty-nine year old Norris. As the man lay bleeding on the floor, Parker fled the building.

Parker wasn't free for long. He was nabbed on May 23 and charged with the murder of Norris. Parker was quickly tried and sentenced to death.

On June 3, 1898, Parker was led up the steps of the wooden gallows to pay for his crimes with his life. In the moments before his life was to end, Parker asked the jailer to tell the other prisoners that he had "died game and like a man." He wanted everyone to know he had been brave while facing his death.

With that, the black hood was placed over Parker's head, and the rope was secured around his neck. After a few painful moments, the execution was over. Parker's body was quietly laid to rest in the Citizens Cemetery.

Fascinating story, right? But what does it have to do with the Tis Art Gallery? Great question!

You see, many think the spirit of James Fleming Parker does not rest peacefully in his grave on Sheldon Street. It is believed that the strange happenings in the building are actually the restless spirit of Parker, attempting to make amends with the man he murdered back in 1897.

Just as it does today, the building had law offices in it when it was built in 1895. Back then, it was known as the Hawkins-Richards Building after the lawyers who built it. Erasmus Lee Norris was one of the lawyers who had an office in the building.

There are many who believe the spirit that haunts the building is James Fleming Parker. Witnesses have claimed to see a ghostly figure at the top of the staircase. The murdered lawyer's office was on the second floor. Is that shadowy figure spotted near the stairwell Parker making his way to Norris's office?

It is said that the elevator opens and closes on its own, with no mechanical explanation for it operating without human intervention. Employees in the law offices claim items move around their work spaces, only to show up again in unexpected spots. One frightened office worker even reported seeing the ghostly face of a man staring at her from outside a second story window. Was that the spirit of Parker, once again trying to find Norris?

It is likely that Parker's unfinished business keeps him tied to the historic building. When things got a bit too spooky for people who had offices in the building, a priest was invited to bless the building. He went from floor to floor, saying prayers and sprinkling holy water. That seemed to do the trick, at least for a little while. The paranormal activity lessened after the priest visited, but something otherworldly remains in that tall building on Cortez Street.

Will Parker's spirit ever rest? Would the murdered Norris accept Parker's apology, even if he was able? And most importantly, what will it take for Parker to cross over to the other side, and face whatever it is that awaits him?

Hassayampa Inn

Beware of Room 426

The Hassayampa Inn, which stands at 122 East Gurley Street, was built in 1927. It is named after the famous Hassayampa River that starts just south of Prescott. Some consider it to be one of the most haunted buildings in Prescott. Once you read about the strange happenings that take place inside its walls, you'll see why!

It's quite possible the hotel is home to ghosts who never actually stayed at the

Hassayampa Inn while they were alive. The Hassayampa is not the first hotel to be built on the land on Gurley Street. The Congress Hotel once stood on this site, but it burned down in 1924. Newspaper accounts from 1924 claim that all twenty-four guests made it out of the fire alive. But did everyone in the building really escape? Not according to local ghost guide Darlene Wilson.

Signs of restless spirits thought to be from the Congress Hotel have been reported in the basement of the Hassayampa Inn. Employees say that at three in the morning, they can hear the sound of many people running down the hall near the housekeeping department, despite the hallways being empty. Those

who have heard the sound describe it as a "stampede of people." Wilson once had the opportunity to take a group of paranormal investigators into the basement of the hotel to see for themselves just what happens in those early morning hours.

When the ghost guide and her group were in the basement waiting to hear the commotion, Darlene Wilson felt a tap on her shoulder. The touch she felt was not from a living being. It was from a ghost. The spirit told her that his name was Silas and that he was a miner who died in the Congress Hotel fire.

After this spine-tingling otherworldly encounter, Wilson did some research on the Congress Hotel. She discovered that the fire in the hotel started at three in the morning. This could explain the sound of people running at exactly that time!

Wilson believes at least three of the hotel's many otherworldly occupants are connected to the fire that destroyed the Congress Hotel.

But not all of the ghosts that linger in this hotel are attached to the Congress. The Hassayampa Inn has plenty of its own ghosts.

Perhaps the most famous ghost that dwells in the hotel is known as Faith Summers. Legend states that Faith and her husband were staying in Room 426 while on their honeymoon. During their stay, Faith's husband left the room to make a quick trip to the store. He never returned.

The new bride spent a few frantic days in the hotel waiting for her husband to come back. But he never did. Overcome with grief, she ended her life in the hotel.

While this popular legend has been told for nearly one hundred years, there is no proof Faith Summers ever stayed in the hotel. But wait! Before you dismiss this as just another made-up ghost story, you should know there are many reports of paranormal activity in Room 426.

Many who visit the room smell the scent of old-fashioned perfume. The aroma is a light, flowery scent that is no longer sold these days, but one that was popular when Faith Summers was supposed to be a guest at the hotel. Housekeeping has tried many things to remove the scent from the room, but each time they do, the flowery perfume smell returns. Are people's noses detecting the presence of Faith, even though their eyes cannot see her?

Local ghost guide Darlene Wilson had a strange paranormal experience in Room 426. She was telling the story of Faith Summers while inside the room. As she was telling the story, she felt something tug at her pant leg. At that moment, one of the people on the ghost tour took a photo, which happened to include Darlene's leg. Unbelievably, the photo captured an orb near Darlene's leg, which no one had seen at the time. Orbs are balls of light that show up in photographs, but sometimes cannot be seen with the naked eye. There are some who believe those bright balls of light are the spirits that still linger in the earthly realm. Was the orb the camera captured actually a photo of Faith?

Darlene's experience in the room was strange. But this is hardly the strangest thing that has happened in the haunted hotel room.

Once a paranormal investigator spent the night in Room 426 to experience the ghostly phenomenon for herself. She reported that at one in the morning she was awakened from a sound sleep by every electric item in the room turning on at once. She dashed out of bed to turn off the lights, the radio, the TV, and everything else that mysteriously turned itself on.

As she settled back into the bed, she felt someone, or something, sit down on the bed next to her. She looked over and saw nothing there. She bravely used her leg to scoot the unseen entity off the bed. A few minutes later, she again felt something join her in bed, so she scooted it off the bed one more time.

But this mischievous ghost was not done interacting with the paranormal investigator.

Moments later, she heard the sound of water running in the bathroom. The investigator was getting frightened. When she heard the sound of a glass filling with water, she covered her eyes in fear. Peeking from between her fingers, she saw the water glass hovering in midair. The glass tipped, as if the unseen spirit was going to pour water over the investigator! But then all of a sudden the glass disappeared. And, it seemed, so did the ghost!

After this bone-chilling event, the paranormal investigator was convinced that Room 426 is haunted. She is not the only one. Many psychics have been to the hotel to visit the famous room. They often report that the energy in the room makes it seems as if a violent death occurred there.

So, is it Faith Summers who is causing all of the unearthly activity in the room? Or did someone else come to a gruesome end in Room 426.

No one knows for certain, but most people agree that *something* haunts that room.

Another well-known ghostly presence in the hotel is a spirit that is known as the Night Watchman. The man, clad in a brown coat, is seen in the lobby. He has been spotted by many of the hotel staff. Late one night, an employee saw the man seated in the darkened lobby. She asked the man if he wanted her to turn on the lobby lights. When he didn't respond, she flipped on the light switch. As light flooded the room, she saw the man had disappeared. It was impossible! There was nowhere for the man to have gone. It was then she realized she had just seen the Night Watchman!

Strange things happen in just about every corner of the beautiful, historic hotel. A group of paranormal tourists reported hearing the sound of a disembodied exhale. Others in the same group said they heard a goosebump-inducing growl come from a darkened corner. Some tourists even saw shadow figures in the hotel.

It is not just paranormal investigators who have strange experiences in the hotel. Hotel guests regularly report eerie happenings

like doors opening and closing on their own, disembodied footsteps, and toothbrushes being moved. Maybe the most unexplainable event of all is the reports of clock radio alarms going off, despite being unplugged from the wall. How is that possible?

With all of the otherworldly happenings that occur inside Hassayampa Inn, it is not hard to understand why it has such a spooky reputation. You might think you are brave, but are you brave enough to check in and encounter what lurks inside this historic hotel?

The (Very) Haunted Hotel Vendome

You are likely to get a wary look if you mention the Hotel Vendome to a Prescott local. The hotel at 230 South Cortez Street is considered by many to be one of the most haunted places in the city—and for good reason! The old building has been making spines shiver since it was built in 1917.

The legend that swirls around the red brick hotel is a terrible one. Storytellers claim that the hotel was once owned by the Byr family. The couple had financial problems that caused them to lose ownership of the hotel.

The new owners of the Hotel Vendome took pity on the couple. They allowed the Byrs to continue to stay at the hotel so they would not be homeless. The couple settled into Room 16.

Then, in 1922, Abigail (Abby) Byr was infected with tuberculosis, also known as TB. The bacterial infection causes the lungs to fill with fluid. The disease causes painful coughing and a fever, as well as other flu-like symptoms. Before a cure for the contagious disease was found, millions of Americans died from TB.

Abby was too ill to leave her bed. Her husband left Room 16 and went to get medicine to ease her cough. The sick woman stayed in bed with her beloved cat, named Noble, curled up at her side. She stroked the cat's fur while she waited for her husband to return.

Abby watched the clock as the minutes turned into hours. She fell asleep waiting for her husband to return to Room 16 with the medicine that would ease her pain and fever. When Abby awoke the next day, she was still all alone in the room. She and her cat stared at the door of the hotel room, waiting for the doorknob to turn and her husband to enter the room with some strange tale explaining how and why he got delayed.

Days passed and the doorknob had still not turned. Abby finally realized that her husband was not going to return. Deathly ill and abandoned, Abby Byr made a terrible choice.

Perhaps she was overcome by the high fever, or maybe it was something else we'll never understand. But she locked her beloved cat Noble in the closet of the hotel room. She then locked the door to Room 16 one final time.

No one went in or out of Room 16 for well over a week. The hotel staff thought it was strange, so they decided to investigate. Once they entered the room, they were likely overcome with the putrid smell of death. Both Abby and Noble were still in the room. They both died of starvation.

Legend has it that Abby and Noble still haunt the hotel where they lived out their final, agonizing days.

It's the hotel's most popular ghost story. The only problem is, there is not much proof that it actually happened. So, if that is not the story, what is? The truth is no one really knows. But there sure is a lot of evidence that something otherworldly has made its home in Room 16.

Ghost hunters and paranormal enthusiasts flock to the room in hopes of having a supernatural encounter of their own.

One disappointed ghost hunter did not get the ghostly encounter she hoped for during her stay in the infamous room. It was suggested that the woman sleep with a saucer of cream in the room on her final night in the hotel. It was thought the treat might tempt the ghostly cat to show itself. She put out the cream and went to sleep, not expecting anything to happen. Unbelievably, she awoke at two thirty in the morning to the ghostly paws of an unseen cat kneading her shoulders.

It is not the only time the otherworldly cat has made itself known in the room. One ghost hunter caught a ghostly cat chasing a ghostly mouse on camera! Another time, the loud meows of a cat were captured on a recording device. Many guests have reported feeling a cat jump on the bed. Others swear they have heard the sounds of a cat scratching on the closet door. Visitors have even been woken from a deep sleep by the sounds of a scampering entity batting around unseen cat toys.

It may not be Noble, but there seems to be enough evidence to suggest that a ghostly cat calls the hotel its home.

Does Abby ever make an appearance? Some people believe she does.

There was a couple who booked Room 16 in hopes of recording evidence of Abby Byr. They would go to bed at their usual time and set

their alarms for two in the morning in hopes the spirits would be more likely to appear while most of the living were fast asleep. Then they'd leap out of bed and turn on their equipment in hopes of capturing a glimpse of Abby. The couple did this several nights in a row, but each time they were unsuccessful.

Their eagerness to interact with the elusive Abby might have driven the spirit out of Room 16. The next morning, they heard the guests in Room 17 report that they heard a woman's voice coming from the darkness of their hotel room. They could see nothing, but the heard

the voice repeat, over and over again, "They just won't leave. They just won't leave." Might that have been the voice of Abby, frustrated by the hotel guests eager to record her?

If you believe the tales, Abby and Noble are not the only ghosts that dwell at the Vendome Hotel.

A cowboy is also spending the afterlife in the hotel. The shadow of a man in a Stetson hat has been spotted several times in the hotel. A staff member was helping guests in Room 3 when she glanced out the door. She saw the

shadow of the cowboy move across the wall in the hallway—but the hallway was empty!

The shadow of the cowboy was also observed by a thirsty ghost hunter who visited the hotel. Late one night the man got out of bed to get a glass of water. As he was making his way downstairs, he noticed the shadow of the cowboy in the hallway. The dark figure silently moved down the hallway in the direction of Rooms 14 and 15.

Who is the cowboy? A medium may have the answer.

A visitor who said she had the ability to communicate with spirits felt drawn to Rooms 14 and 15, and asked the staff if she could spend some time there. She was in the rooms for about thirty minutes. When she emerged, she said she believed years ago a cowboy was staying in Room 14 and fell in love with a woman staying in Room 15. The shy cowboy never told the woman how he felt about her, but the medium thinks his actions may have shown how he felt.

She sensed that he'd spend nights on a chair outside her window, keeping guard over the woman. Perhaps he was concerned about the lady being alone in the wild and rowdy frontier town?

It seems another medium also sensed the cowboy. A talented psychic, who never visited the hotel, or heard any of its ghostly tales, was shown a photo of the hotel lobby. The photo showed two glowing orbs hovering in the middle of the image.

The medium focused on the image for a long time. She then declared the orbs were spirits, one was a cowboy, and the other was a woman. Did she identify the cowboy and Abby? How could she have known about them?

With all of the strange, otherworldly happenings in the hotel, it is easy to understand how the hotel became known as one of the town's most haunted buildings. Ghost hunters from all over come to the Hotel Vendome, eager to have their own ghostly encounter. Will you dare to be among them? If you are, beware of any cats you find curling around your leg. . .

Hotel St. Michael

CHAPTER 9

Hotel St. Michael Is (Not) Haunted

What would you do if you were a ghost in a building that people insist isn't haunted? That is the predicament of the ghosts that call the Hotel St. Michael their home. If you stop in at the front desk of the red brick hotel and ask the person behind the counter if the hotel is haunted, they will probably tell you that there are no otherworldly spirits there.

But there are some guests of the hotel, located on 205 West Gurley Street, who are certain that they have had paranormal experiences in the hotel.

It is easy to come up with reasonable explanations for some of what these guests have seen, heard, and smelled. There are people who have stayed in the hotel who describe hearing the sound of footsteps in empty hallways. Others have claimed to smell the scent of perfume from a bygone era lingering in empty rooms. These experiences are intriguing, but a skeptic who doesn't believe in ghosts might dismiss them as nothing more than the result of many people coming and going in a busy hotel.

While those may be easy events to explain away, there are some paranormal reports that are a little more difficult to make sense of.

There are accounts of ghostly children who play in the guest elevator. Late at night, when most guests are asleep, the sounds of giggling children have been heard from the elevator shaft. The elevator will travel from floor to floor, and when the doors slide open, no one is there. The doors then close, and the game continues into the night.

If ghosts in the elevator seem hard to explain, this next story is sure to top it. It is hard to understand how this experience is anything other than a supernatural event.

The strange experience happened in Room 228. A couple was staying in the room, and about an hour after they checked in, they heard a knock at the door. The man got up to see who it was, but before he could get there, the locked door flung open.

A young woman stood in the doorway. She asked to speak with a certain person. The couple said this person was not in the room. Before the visitors could get more information from the mysterious woman, she closed the door.

The man immediately opened the door to talk with the woman. He looked down the hall, but it was empty. Whoever this woman was, she seemed to have vanished into thin air.

The couple were concerned that the woman was able to enter their locked hotel room, so they went down to the front desk to ask for help. When they told the lobby clerk what just occurred, the couple was told that what they had described wasn't possible.

There was only one key to the room and the couple had it in their possession. No one could have entered their locked room.

Still puzzled as to how the woman was able to open the locked door, they walked back to Room 228. As soon as they entered the room, it was clear that someone, or something, had been in the room while they were gone.

The moment they opened the door, icy air hit their skin. The window in the room, which had been closed when they went to the lobby, was now wide open and cold gusts of January air were blowing in. As they rushed over to close the window, they also noticed the air conditioner was whirring. It was set to 55 degrees. They quickly shut it off. Who had been in the room and why did they want it so cold?

How had a woman entered Room 228 without a key? A skeptic might say the woman worked at the hotel and she had mistakenly entered the room. But, if it had been housekeeping or another hotel staff member, why would she open the window and turn on the air conditioner, especially since it was the middle of winter?

Do you have any ideas on what happened in Room 228? If it isn't otherworldly, what could it possibly be?

Is the Hotel St. Michael haunted? It depends on who you ask. But, to be on the safe side, if you decide to stay at the hotel, I would recommend you avoid the elevators late at night. And, of course, stay away from Room 228. That is, unless you want to see for yourself if this hotel really IS haunted.

CHAPTER 10

Gone, But Not Forgotten

In the 1800s, the settlers who came to this area were tough men and women who carved a life out of the desert. They dug mines, drove cattle, and established towns with little more than hard work and determination.

But what happened when the cowboys, bandits, prospectors, and other Arizona pioneers grew so old they needed help looking after themselves? Some of those early trailblazers made their final home address 300 South McCormick Street, the site of the Arizona Pioneers' Home.

When the home opened in 1911, it could house up to forty men. The men were required to be at least sixty years old, and they had to have lived in the Arizona territory for at least twenty-five years. In 1916, the home began to welcome women residents. In 1927, the home opened its doors to disabled miners, as well as the elderly.

Over the years, many people important to the Grand Canyon State's history lived in the home. Former politicians, businessmen, artists, and even Prescott's own Sharlot Hall (who you'll meet in the next chapter) lived in the building at some point. Perhaps the most famous person to reside in the Arizona Pioneers' Home is Mary Katherine Horony Cummings. If the name doesn't sound familiar to you, maybe you know her by her nickname. They called her "Big Nose Kate."

Kate became part of Wild West history when she met John Henry Holliday. People called him Doc Holliday because he was a dentist, but he is best known as a gambler and gunfighter. Kate and Doc made their home in Tombstone in 1880. They cemented their place in history when Holliday fought alongside Wyatt Earp and his brothers in the famous gunfight at the O.K. Corral on October 20, 1881. Holliday had contracted TB when he was younger, and he died from the disease in November, 1887. He was only thirty-six years old.

Kate was a different story. She spent her golden years in the home and took her final breath inside its walls on November 2, 1940.

Today, the Arizona Pioneers' Home has 150 residents. Well, living residents, anyway.

Many who spend time in the home late at

night claim to hear the sounds of disembodied footsteps throughout the building. The sound of someone walking echoes in the empty hallways, but no soul can be seen. Who is it that continues to roam the building long after death?

It could be that the ghostly late-night walker also enjoys watching television. An employee of the home tells a strange story of an event that occurred in the resident's TV lounge. A group of residents gathered in the room to watch a movie together. When the show was over, the residents went back to their rooms and went to bed.

The employee noticed the television was left on in the now empty lounge, so she walked over to the TV and shut it off. As she turned to walk out of the room, the TV turned itself back on. Puzzled, the employee returned to the TV, and once again, turned it off . She had only taken a few steps when, once again, the TV powered itself on!

Frustrated, the employee reached behind the TV and unplugged it from the wall. Without electricity, the TV certainly would not be able to turn itself on. As she peered behind the TV set she made a chilling discovery.

The TV was already unplugged. How was it able to turn itself on if it had never been plugged in to begin with?

We may never know who the spirit is that makes itself known in the Arizona Pioneers' Home, but it seems certain in life the person loved Arizona so much that even in death, the Grand Canyon state is preferred to whatever lies on the other side.

Sharlot Hall Museum

The Home that Sharlot Saved

Sharlot Hall Museum is named for Sharlot Mabridth Hall. Born in Kansas in 1870, she came to the Arizona Territory as a child and fell in love with her new home. She also loved stories and gathered tales from the Arizona pioneers.

When Sharlot was older, she campaigned for Arizona statehood. She worked hard to preserve the history of the Arizona Territory and Prescott, which had been the capital of the Arizona Territory. Sharlot started that work with the old Governor's Mansion.

In 1864, a four-room log cabin was built for Arizona Territory's first governor, John M. Goodwin, and the Secretary of the Territory, Richard C. McCormick. They lived here while the government was being established. The log cabin became the Governor's Mansion and was used until 1867, when Tucson became the capital of the territory.

After that the log cabin was used as a private home, then a boarding house, and even a laundry! Sharlot Hall was not happy about this. She wanted people to remember how important the log cabin was to the history of the state.

Sharlot was determined to preserve the building, and her hard work paid off. In 1927, the City of Prescott bought the log cabin and let Sharlot turn it into a museum. And she lived in the museum she loved until she died in 1943. After that, others who believed in her dream took over the museum.

The museum has grown over the years. The block-long site now includes not only the Governor's Mansion, but also an amphitheater, several historic homes, and Fort Misery.

Over the years, there have been whisperings that spirits still linger in the old Governor's Mansion. Psychics who visit the property claim to sense ghosts in the building. Employees have reported seeing shapes and shadows, only to have the objects quickly drift from view. Some are certain a spirit is responsible for moving objects around the museum. It is not uncommon for something to disappear, only to be found later in an unexpected location. Those who have experienced the mysteriously moved objects are certain no one in the museum is responsible the relocation of the items. At least, no one who is among the living.

Once, an assistant archivist working at her desk saw a woman out of the corner of her eye. The well-dressed woman walked past the archivist's desk, and the employee stood up to speak to her. When she turned to the greet the woman, no one was there. The woman the archivist saw had disappeared without a trace!

Who could this otherworldly entity be? Some think it is Sharlot Hall herself. They believe she continues to keep a watchful eye on the building she worked so hard to preserve. Others say the spirit might be Margaret McCormick. Margaret lived in the home after it was built and became the First Lady of the Arizona Territory when her husband became the area's second governor in 1866.

Sadly, Margaret died in childbirth inside the building in 1867. The citizens of Prescott mourned the death of the woman and her baby. At first, Margaret was laid to rest on the grounds, but later her body was sent to be reburied in her hometown of Rahway, New Jersey. Could it be that Margaret's spirit remains in the place where her life ended?

Perhaps the most haunted building on the grounds is Fort Misery. In 2010, a group of paranormal investigators arrived at the museum with a load of ghost hunting equipment that included infrared cameras and EVP recorders, ready to capture evidence of supernatural activity.

The investigative team broke into small groups. One small group, led by museum volunteer Parker Anderson, headed over to Fort Misery to begin their ghost hunt. Once inside the fort, the team turned off the lights in the building to allow their infrared cameras to work better. These cameras are sometimes called "thermal cameras." They work by detecting the presence of heat energy. Using the camera, ghost hunters can see temperature changes that cannot be detected by the human eye.

While the group sat in the dark room, a psychic in the group reported that she saw a ghost. The psychic said she could see a ghostly young woman sitting on the bed that was on display in the fort. No one else in the room could see the spirit, but they could hear the psychic speaking to the ghostly woman.

The psychic told the rest of the group that the young woman was waiting in the fort to be reunited with her love. The spirit was waiting for the man to come back and lead her into the other side. The psychic tried to explain to the ghostly woman that her love was already on the other side and waiting for her to cross over. The ghost did not believe the psychic. She was determined to wait to be led to the other side, no matter what the psychic told her. They could not help the spirit to cross over that night.

The group left Fort Misery with an interesting story to tell the other paranormal investigators in their group. Anderson recalls, to his dismay, the psychic did not ask the ghost for her name, when she died, or any other details that would help him discover the identity of the spirit. The mysterious encounter left the group with more questions than answers.

Whether you are looking for history or ghosts, it seems as if the Sharlot Hall Museum has plenty of both! Next time you are there, keep a watchful eye out for any well-dressed women drifting through the Governor's Mansion. It just might be a famous woman from Arizona's past!

And, if I were you, I'd make sure the lights were on while inside Fort Misery...

Fort Whipple Museum

One Last Dance

Have you been to the Fort Whipple Museum? Today, the wooden building can be found on the grounds of the Veterans Administration Hospital and is part of the Sharlot Hall Museum. It might look small, but it played a BIG role in Arizona history! The property has been used by the military since 1864 and was once, for a short time, Arizona's territorial capital.

Legend has it that the spirit of a young woman haunts Fort Whipple. She was the daughter of a colonel who oversaw the fort long ago. When her family lived on the property there were few women in Prescott. Because young ladies were such a rarity, the girl got a great deal of attention from the soldiers. And she enjoyed the attention!

The colonel's daughter came to each ball that was hosted on the property. Her dance card was always full. All eyes were on the lovely young woman as she twirled around the dance floor in her beautiful gowns. She captured the hearts of many of the soldiers, but few could win her affection. She enjoyed being courted by her many suitors and did not want to have a serious relationship with any of soldiers yearning for her attention.

Based on the sightings of this ghostly young woman, it appears she is still searching Fort

Whipple for the young man who will capture her heart.

At one time, she was the belle of the ball, and in the afterlife, maybe she longs to recapture those exciting times? It could be why her spirit remains in the building. Who knows, perhaps if you play a tune when you visit, you may see the otherworldly form of the colonel's daughter twirl across the room one more time.

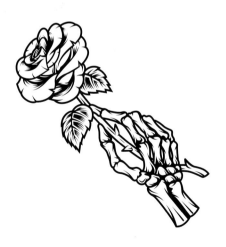

Anna Lardinois tingles the spines of Milwaukee locals and visitors through her haunted, historical walking tours known as Gothic Milwaukee. The former English teacher is an ardent collector of stories, an avid walker, and a sweet treat enthusiast. She happily resides in a historic home in Milwaukee that, at this time, does not appear to be haunted.

Check out some of the other Spooky America titles available now!

Spooky America was adapted from the creeptastic Haunted America series for adults. Haunted America explores historical haunts in cities and regions across America. Each book chronicles both the widely known and less-familiar history behind local ghosts and other unexplained mysteries. Here's more from *Haunted Prescott* authors Darlene Wilson and Parker Anderson:

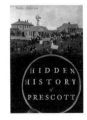
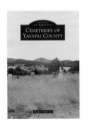